The Legend of "Chicken Hill"

in Pottstown, PA

WRITTEN BY: ARSONIA M. LEISURE

ISBN 978-0-7414-2392-4

Published by:

INFINITY
PUBLISHING.COM

1094 New DeHaven Street, Suite 100
West Conshohocken, PA 19428-2713
Info@buybooksontheweb.com
www.buybooksontheweb.com
Toll-free (877) BUY BOOK
Local Phone (610) 941-9999
Fax (610) 941-9959

Printed in the United States of America

Published December 2013

FOREWORD

This story unfolds in a small close knit community in the borough of Pottstown, Pennsylvania, Montgomery County, approximately nineteen (19) miles from Reading, Pa. and thirty-eight (38) miles from the city of Philadelphia, Pa.

This legend chronicles people living in the "Chicken Hill" section of town. This story covers a span of time after the Depression of 1929 (and continues with a synopsis of the story of the author's life). It has been said that people lost their life savings when this depression fell upon them, because banks failed. This story may be ambiguous to you. The narration will leave much to one's own imagination as you will see.

This book will be quite enjoyable to people of all ages–adolescents and adults, in particular. It is intrinsic that this story is being shared with you. During this time, families had a most difficult time raising their families due to the scarcity of food and money.

However, it was amazing the camaraderie that existed among the families in those days. This is a story about Rev. and Mrs. Isaiah Glenn and some of their children. However, not all of their children appear in this story, because they were too young to contribute to the story. I played with my brothers, because they were closer to my age, two sisters were older and one sister much younger. You have now been invited to share this story with a lady that has lived in that section of town, all of her entire life. She calls to her remembrance her story which she has named, "The Legend of Chicken Hill". This story will surprise many of you. However, we hope it will inspire you to tell others about the events that did happen after the Depression of 1929.

This is the story about Arsonia M. (Glenn) Leisure. Arsonia said, “This is the place where I “hopped, “skipped”, “jumped”, and “played”, until I was so tired,–this is the place where I expect that I will eventually die.” Change has a lot to do with the outcome of our daily lives. There are the things that a family is expected to do in controlling their children. Then there are the things that society must do to help us maintain that control. Our government has a greater control over what we should allow to come into our communities. They must control the borders to keep infestations out of our lives. Infestations breed diseases that can become a breeding ground for many of our addictions.

We trust them to control the larger part of those problems before they get into our societies. We love our country, and we work toward the betterment of our country, and we expect our country to protect our lives and not let deleterious infiltration bring harm to us as we all work together for justice and equality for all humanities.

DEDICATION

I am dedicating this book to my beloved, sister
Loretta
Who left much too early from our lives

Besides being my sister, she was a true friend
She also was the backbone and support for me
in times of trouble–in times of sorrow

I miss her immensely, and I look forward to rejoining her
eternally, someday, over there

Now that you're living somewhere between
the moon and the stars

Someday

I'll get to where you are–I will, Loretta

I will

"Sonia"

ABOUT THE BOOK

This is a non-fiction book. All of the stories about persons and events that took place in this book are true. Any similarities or circumstances that may appear in likeness to anyone living now, or dead, would be purely coincidental. In the mid 1900's, World War I was going on, and the United States and Germany were involved in this war. Germany was under the dictatorship of Adolf Hitler who had millions of Jewish people annihilated under his absolute controlling authority. People called DP's (displaced persons) were placed in concentration camps. Women were horribly tortured, and men were purposely damaged so that they would never be able to produce a child. Of course, others scrambled to get to the DMZ (demilitarized zones) which were the areas free of military control, in an effort to defect to a free country as an asylum from the political atrocities dealt to them and their children. Even their children were separated from their families–never to be seen again.

This was a despicable and dastardly act, indeed! The Depression of 1929 caused the Stock Market to then "crash". However, it wasn't until the Japanese pulled a "sneak attack" and bombed Pearl Harbor, in the Philippines on December 7, 1941 that we were brought into World War II. This attack forced us to declare war on the Japanese and drop the Atomic Bomb on them in Hiroshima and in Okinawa.

I recalled that a newspaper was handed out one morning saying "V" day (meaning victory day). I remember people running out screaming, "The war is over!" "The war is over!" Then came the "tolling" of the church bells all over Pottstown–ringing out that the war was finally over. My understanding of it all was vague, but I could feel the happiness in our home and throughout the area where we lived which led me to believe that something great had happened. I was able to grasp, in my mind, that there would be no more killing of people. This prompted me to write this book in an effort to promote the awareness of the things that happened during wartime in the U. S., in the town where I lived with my parents and family.

Today was a beautiful crisp day. The flowers were blooming and the trees were just beginning to bud. It was quite windy, and you know what that meant to us. I called my brothers and neighbors together and said, “Come on let’s get together and make some kites.” I said, “I’ll go in the house and look for some newspapers and also some rags for the tails.” Luckily, we still had some rags put away in the cellar. The “Rag Man” hadn’t picked them up, yet. We saved all of our rags for him. We packed the newspapers in bundles for him. You received only a minimal amount of money for your rags and newspapers.

Each one of us cut our newspapers in a diamond shape and attached them to sticks that were perpendicular to form the frame. We hung the string in the center of the kite. Then we tied a string and some rags on the bottom of our kite to make a tail. We would get a running start, and then we let it go. She soared up into the air helped by the wind. She soared like an eagle. It was so much fun!

Sometimes we would run up to the Jefferson playground to fly our kites. We could run off of the dirt mound there to get a good running start to fly our kites. Usually the rest of the kids would follow suit and come together with us to enjoy the fun. Later in the day, we went back down the street, from the Jefferson School. It started to rain, and then we heard the thunder. We saw a flash of lightning. We rushed to get a piece of metal from the garbage can. It was the top of a discarded sardine can. We wanted to see if we could accomplish what Benjamin Franklin did. We got caught and we were reprimanded and told to get in the house. My Mom said, “Don’t you kids know you’ll get electrocuted and die doing that!” So much for copying Benjamin Franklin–for today, anyway.

Nightfall has now come and we had to get into the house. We ate our supper, and we had just a little more time to sit around and talk with each other. We always sat together at the table to talk about the things that happened that day. You heard everything while you were sitting at the dinner table. We had just finished doing the dishes and guess what happened? We heard, "Whoooooo! Whoooooo!" That was a siren, and we heard the announcement, "Air Raid!" "Everyone in your house!" "Quick, pull down the shades!" "Turn on the red lamps!" "Everyone sit down and be quiet until the 'Air Raid' is over." Our country was at war, and there was a threat of our getting "bombed". All of us usually ran into the corner of our parlor and sat on the floor. Of course, it usually happened at night and sometimes while I was in school. My best friend, Bernadette, always "threw up" when she heard the call for an "Air Raid". She said her mother would always rush her to the bathing area to throw up. After a short time passed, a man came down the street yelling, "All clear, all clear!" We could now pull up the shades and turn on the lights. We did not have television. Our connection to the outside world was the newspapers and magazines. However, the radio stations ranged from here to as far away as Czechoslovakia, Germany and the like. We had keen, inventive and inquisitive minds. Many adult occurrences remained "closed doors" to the youth.

Yes, our connection to the outside world was the newspapers, magazines, and also the radio. We listened to the following stories on the radio. We had to use our minds to engulf ourselves into the stories to determine and to envision what was going on in the series. The reason was that the stories had a time limit and were ongoing each day–never ending. Therefore, you had to tune in every day to find out what was going on. Some of the stories that we listened to were as follows: The Lone Ranger & Tonto, Fibber McGee and Molly and, of course, The Shadow Knows. At the end of the broadcast, the shadow would say, "Who knows what has entered into the hearts of men?"

"The Shadow knows." ("Ha, Ha, Ha")

Sometimes when we would be listening to our stories on the radio, the delivery man would be bringing the groceries into the house. The store was first owned by the Estreicher family. Later, it was purchased by S&R (Schlosberg & Rubin).

I would like to tell you how we got our groceries in those days. Mom would write her list on a piece of paper–the things that she wanted to buy. When she made out her list, she wrote down the pound weight and/or number of the item that she wanted to purchase. You must understand that there were no comparison of prices. You paid the "going" price for your request. Then they would rewrite her order on a small pad or notebook, listing the price of the items that she requested.

We retained our book, and they kept their copy. This way my Dad knew how much he owed them when it was time to pay the bill. My Dad paid the bill every two (2) weeks. You had to pay the bill faithfully if you wanted to purchase more groceries. You needed to understand that. My Mom worked very hard to prepare the food that we would be eating. I could smell my Mom's cooking a couple blocks away. I remember that very well. The air was much cleaner and purer in those days than they are now.

One thing that most children would not know is the fact that we had an "Ice Man", named Mr. Blanding, to deliver our ice that we needed to keep our food from spoiling. This ice was put in an ice box. Imagine that! He carried a very large round, two-prong fork to carry the ice into the house. He always had to "chip" off the large "cake" of ice to make it fit into the top of the ice box. This was done with an "ice pick". We also used an "ice pick", that we kept in the kitchen, to "chip" off a piece of ice when we wanted to drink a cool glass of water. We used an "old-fashioned" infamous depressed-shaped "tin" cup to hold the water that we wanted to drink. It really worked well, because it would get so cold that we would have to take a piece of cloth and wrap it around the "tin" cup to hold the cup. The ice merely lasted a week–especially in the hot summertime. We lived in a tidy, very well-kept home. Lawns, however, were sparse, and we had to take turns picking up the pebbles and broken glass out of the yard, besides weeding and sweeping the yard whenever necessary. We had a nice front yard pavement at 657 Beech Street, where now sits a borough municipal building. I remember my home. I loved the old homestead. I think about it often.

We used to ride our box cars, tricycles, scooters and wagons up and down our front yard pavement. We had neighbors of different ethnic backgrounds such as Polish, Slovak, Jewish, Pennsylvania Dutch, etc. I learned that the Pennsylvania Dutch, in particular, prepared some excellent dishes on a minimal monetary budget. Dad said, "Those folk can do a lot with so little."

One day we decided to play "Hi Hitler!" My Mom and Dad said, "Oh no you don't!" "He's a terrible man!" "He killed a lot of people!" "Don't you let me ever see you copy anything that man does." "That isn't a game to play!" We immediately stopped playing that game. We didn't even know the man then?

As the day went on, my brother, Dodge said to me, "Let's run away from home." It seemed like a good idea at the time. We walked up Beech St. and turned onto Grant St. We sat down on the curb. Then we smelled a wonderful aroma from down the street. We realized it was Mom's cooking. She was cooking some southern fried chicken, turnip greens and hot yeast rolls. It smelled so good! We said, "Let's not run away today." "Let's do it another day". That was so stupid! We were happy at home, and we loved our parents. How stupid can you be? Trust me, we never tried that again.

Some of the men in Pottstown were called to the Armed Services. My Dad was exempted. They said that he had too many children, and he needed to remain at home with his wife and family. At the time, he was employed at Jacob's Aircraft Company. It was during this time period that the Japanese had bombed Pearl Harbor.

All of the families living here were given ration books, because it was wartime in our country. Food was scarce. Fortunately, we received books for each one of us. From those books you were allowed to purchase such things as I can recall as: butter, flour, cheese, sugar, milk, eggs, etc. You just couldn't "hog up" as much food as you wanted; that's why each person was given this allowance of provision to maintain his/her sustenance. When you needed to purchase certain commodities, your parent would tear out the slip of paper from one of the ration books. Not all food was rationed–just certain things. We may have had it hard in those days, but we were a sharing community. There was no problem with your borrowing a cup of sugar or a portion of butter from your neighbor, and you were not "shunned" for doing so. I remember vividly neighbors returning a couple of eggs or something else. They always returned the item back to you–always! Sometimes I ate at my neighbor's house, and sometimes my neighbor ate at my Mom's house. Then, too, our neighbor would send a portion of cake that she baked over to my Mom's house. She wanted to share with us things she prepared, and my Mom did the same, too. Actually, we told people that we were rich. Well, we didn't know any better?

A funny thing happened one day. Mom baked four beautiful apple pies for dessert. She put them on the broad window ledge to "cool". The next thing that we knew was that the cat jumped up on the window ledge and walked through all our pies.

My Mom was quite upset, and my Father was too, because he knew that my Mother would never serve us those pies. She picked them up from the window ledge and threw them in the garbage can – "depression" or not. My Dad laughed and laughed. We were upset, too. I think my Dad had to relocate the cat at someone else's home after that, because we didn't see it anymore. We were so looking forward to "delving" into Mom's fresh apple pies. So much for apple pie. "Huh?"

We were having a great day, and it was beginning to get late. I was playing with some of my friends. Dad called us and said that it was time for Bible Study. We had weekly prayer services at home. Our friends had a choice. They had to either come into the prayer services with us, or they could choose to go home. They always wanted to stay and share the services with us. O yes, it was my duty (respectfully speaking) to read a certain passage of scripture from the Bible; namely, Matthew 5, verses one to 12. This is known as the "Beatitudes", and I quote:

And seeing the multitudes, he went up into a mountain, and when he was set, his disciples came unto him: And he opened his mouth, and taught them saying,

Blessed are the poor in spirit: for their's is the kingdom of heaven.

Blessed are they that mourn: for they shall be comforted.

Blessed are the meek: for they shall inherit the earth.

Blessed are they which do hunger and thirst after righteousness for they shall be filled.

Blessed are the merciful: for they shall obtain mercy.

Blessed are the pure in heart: for they shall see God.

Blessed are the peacemakers: for they shall be called the children of God.

Blessed are they which are persecuted for righteousness' sake: for their's is the kingdom of heaven

Blessed are ye when men shall revile you, and persecute you, and shall say all manner of evil against you falsely, for my sake.

Rejoice and be exceedingly glad: for great is your reward in heaven: for so persecuted they the prophets which were before you.

I cannot tell you how many times my Dad asked me to read that scripture. However, it is one of my favorite scriptures in the Bible, as of yet. We would sing many different hymns from our Gospel Pearl music book and also our Baptist Hymnal. My father would give the prayer. We would study and go over different parts of the Bible and discuss it.

My brothers would take turns speaking for the Lord. My brother Sage or Dodge would say, "The Lord doesn't want you to tell any lies!" My Dad would say, "Amen." Then they would say, "The Lord doesn't want you to say any bad words." My Dad would again say, "Amen." Then they would say, "The bad words are"—–my Dad would interrupt and say, "We know what they are!" "Get on with it!" My Dad knew very well what my brothers were eluding to, and he wasn't having that–not at all. They were trying to get away with something. After some discussions, and singing of a few more hymns and Dad giving the final prayer, Bible Study was ended until next week.

To continue writing this story I need to tell you why Pottstown was called, "Chicken Hill". In case you haven't guessed by now, people living in this time frame raised chickens to help feed their families. Some of them raised ducks and other fowl, too. Some families had goats. I asked my Dad why they had goats in their yards. "Arsonia, he said, "they have a goat for getting goat's milk." Then he laughed. I said, "I wouldn't drink any goat's milk–no way!" My Dad continued on to say, "Well, just because you don't drink it doesn't mean other people aren't going to drink the goat's milk." "You should try it." "I understand that it tastes good, and that there are some infants that have to drink goat's milk due to their digestive abnormalities that they have."

The Hoover family owned a candy store, after Mr. Kline had it . They had a monkey. Besides buying their candy, we always went up to their store to see their monkey. It must have been a "monkey thing" in those days, because on certain weekends, there was a "monkey grinder" that would come into town. What is a "monkey grinder"? It was a man that carried a square-shaped music box. He would turn the handle on the box, and we would hear music. The monkey sat on the top of the box, jumping around, as the man grinded out his music. The music box was usually red in color, as was the monkey with his little red shirt that he had on, along with his matching little round hat "cocked" to the side of his head. Attached to his hat was a rubber band holding on the little hat on his head. There were a lot of happenings on "Chicken

Hill". "Yes sireeee!" "Chicken Hill" was a panorama of the following streets: Beech St., Sheridan St., Grant St., Lincoln Ave., Warren St., Hale St., Jefferson Ave., and N. Adams St.

Getting back to listening to the radio, let me tell you about some of our favorite stars that we looked forward to hearing on the radio: Lena Horne, Ethel Waters and Marian Anderson.[1] As you may know Marian Anderson was born in the city of Philadelphia, Pa. She was known as the "Baby Contralto". She got 50 cents to sing at church socials. Her contralto voice was one of the sensations of the American concert stage. It was said that her father was an ice and coal vendor, and that her mother took in washing and did house cleaning. Toscanini [2] stated that a voice like hers was heard only once in a lifetime. She was known, also, to speak four languages. We enjoyed listening to the Andrews Sisters. Everyday we listened to Kate Smith singing, "God Bless America". The male singers that we enjoyed were Bing Crosby and Frank Sinatra. There were two famous newscasters that we enjoyed, and they were Walter Winchel whose closing lines were, "Now you heard it from me." John Facenda's closing lines were, "Good Night All." How could you forget about three others that we listened to: George Burns and Gracie Allen, Amos and Andy, and Jack Benny. In addition to Jack Benny being a great comedian, he played the violin exceptionally well–a violin virtuoso, I suppose.

Believe it or not, everyone on the "planet" had a dog or a cat. One day our dog, "Mickey" was due to have her puppies. She was struggling and having a difficult time. We had made a pallet on the cellar floor for her. My Dad stayed down in the cellar with her and aided her in having her puppies. I don't know what my Dad did, but finally he hollered,"You can come down to the cellar now!" "Mickey" had her puppies!" We were "flabbergasted".

It was time for us to have our "inoculations". The doctor came to our house in those days. Nowadays they call "inoculations" immunizations. The doctor would wait until everyone

---

[1] ibid. Life Magazine, page 20, 22 ed. February 22, 1937
[2] op.cit (Toscanini, Arturo 1867 - 1957) Orchestra Conductor was born in Italy.

was in bed. My Mom would then bring him upstairs to our bedroom. I well remember the family doctor. His name was Dr. John Sherbon. He took very good care of us. We went to see him at the funeral parlor (That's what they used to call it) when he passed away. We were greatly saddened at his passing. We had to then rely on Dr. Harry Marcy and Dr. David Detar for our care.

I always said that we built up antibodies in our bodies. Why do I say this? You won't believe this, but my oldest sister, Berwindale would chew her chewing gum for awhile; and then she would give it to my sister, Loretta, and she would chew it for awhile. When she got tired of it, she would put it into my mouth, and I would chew it for awhile. When I got tired of it, I just stuck it on the curb on Beech St. Any chewing gum that I placed on the curb back in the 1940's has since disintegrated for sure. We, however, did not share our gum with our brothers–just we three sisters. You know, "It was a sister thing." Oh, yes, we did share the glass of water with them, though–not like today. Children today will not drink after each other anymore. Well, we survived. That's the main thing. We were healthy children, and we were disease free. Industrial plants were not as rampart as they are today, I suppose.

By the way, you could smell lightning bugs. We used to "squeeze" off the lighted part of the lightning bug, put it in a jar, and use it as a way to light our way in getting home at night. Can you truly believe that! Oh that's nothing! We used to catch the "June bug", and put it in a jar with grass lined at the bottom of the jar. We would punch holes in the metal lid to give the bug some air to breathe. Then we would just sit down and watch it to see what it did. Oh yes, the "grasshopper"–we put him in a jar and did the same thing to him, too. I believe he must have chewed tobacco or something, because we saw some black stuff in the jar (smile). I don't know where that came from.

Once we saw a turtle crossing the street (very little traffic in those days). We ran and picked it up. My brothers took it from me. They said, "Watch out–give it here!" "It'll bite off your finger!" "He might be a "snapping turtle"! I didn't know a "snapping turtle" from any other turtle. So, I just let them be in charge of that. I just decided to play with the "caterpillar". I was wondering how long it would take for it to turn into a "butterfly". I figured it would be quite a while yet, so I just sat her down on the outside window ledge of our cellar. Did you know that you can also smell June bugs, caterpillars and things? Sometimes you can even smell a snake. It smells like "watermelon". Oooh!

You could smell the breeze rippling through the trees, and you could smell the peppermint plants, tea leaves and dandelions popping out everywhere! Many of our neighbors cooked dandelions. They would be picking them from the fields everywhere. I never tried to taste them to see if I liked them. I probably should have. In fact, I wished now that I had tried to taste some. Let's not forget the smell of lilacs, honeysuckle and roses in our yards, as well as the pansies and sunflowers. My favorite flowers then were the buttercups and the violets. They were very small flowers, but attractive to me. Many of these flowers grew in our neighbors' yards, too. Planting flowers was a major attraction in people's lives.

By the way, in speaking about tea and/or tea plants, you probably didn't know that when you made tea, you had to boil the leaves and then use a "tea strainer" to hold back the tea leaves from the liquid. Then you discarded the tea leaves when you got all the tea strained out that you needed for a cup of hot tea or iced tea with lemon, for instance.

When we bought something from the store and opened up our purchase, we placed our wrapper in the receptacle there at the store. If you were walking down the street and took the wrapper off of your purchase, you took the wrapper home with you and discarded it there. You did not see wrappings from things purchased from a store and/or restaurant all over the streets like you do now. We were never allowed to do anything like that! When I see people do that now, I "cringe". It really gets my "mitigated gall" It really does!

Later on came the wringer-washer machine that was used to wash our clothes. Yes, it was an electric appliance that moved your clothes around similar to an automatic washer, except that you put each piece of clothing that you washed through a wringer (two moving rollers) to wring the water out of your clothes. Then you put the clothes in a large tub to rinse out the soap suds. We put something called "blue-ing" in the rinse out tub to make our clothes look cleaner and whiter. There was another tub to put the clothes in that needed starch. Oh you don't know what starch is? Well it was a component of white, tasteless, solid, chemical carbohydrate in the form of minute granules found in plants such as rice, corn, wheat, beans, potatoes, etc. You mixed it with cold water and then cooked it slowly on the stove until it became a smooth texture. You dipped your clothes in it, and then hung the clothes outside to dry. You had to hang your clothes outside in the summer as well as in the winter. There were no automatic dryers, you see.

After the clothes were dry, you sprinkled your clothes with water and used a heated iron that you placed on the coal stove to get warm enough to iron out the wrinkles from your clothes. Later on when your home was installed with electricity, you plugged your iron into the wall socket after connecting a removable plug to the iron. For the clothes that were "heavily soiled, you used a washboard to clean those clothes. What was a washboard? It was a frame with a corrugated metallic or other surface on which clothes were rubbed while in the process of washing. There was no such thing as permanent pressed clothes–no way! You think you have it hard now? "Ooooh!" Besides all this, they had to take the rugs outside to beat the dust out of them–no vacuum cleaners? By the way, one day, Sage accidentally caught his arm in the wringer of the washer, and it broke his arm. He had to wear a cast on it for awhile.

Now I know you played jacks. What's jacks? It's throwing down a hand full of metal spikes on a table to see how many of them you could grab immediately after bouncing a small red ball on the same table. The game is still around today. That game called for precision and timing in order to win.

On Saturdays, on Sheridan St., there was an elderly lady by the name of Mrs. Yergey. She owned a store at the corner of Sheridan and Beech Sts. We would all go there for Bible Study. We always brought along what few pennies that we had to buy our candy after Bible Study. She had an array of different kinds of candies. I think that's why so many children came to her Bible Study. Uh-huh? The kinds of condiments that she sold were: peppermint sticks, candy canes, bubble gum, sugar babies, cookies, cracker jacks, lemon, lime, orange gum drops and watermelon slices, licorice that was red, black or brown and cinnamon candy. She also had candies of all flavors, all kinds of rippled (wavy-like) candies. She also had jaw breakers. Jaw breakers ruined your teeth. We bought the licorice so that we could chew it and spit it out like the old folks did when they were "chewing tobacco" When they chewed tobacco, they held it in their cheeks; Then they would "spit" out the juice. When they "dipped snuff", they chewed it and held it in their inside chin pocket with their tongue. After they grew tired of their "chewing tobacco" or "dipping snuff", they just simply discarded it.

Don't you dare forget about all the pennies we spent on candy cigarettes. We loved them!

That made us feel grown–that's all. Remember them? Let's not forget about all those "fire crackers" that we bought for our "cap guns" that we wore in our holsters. We played cowboys everyday. We would pull the "trigger" of our cap guns just to hear the "popping" sounds. We just loved "Hopalong Cassidy", Tom Mix, Gene Autry, Roy Rogers and Dale Evans, and how could we forget the Lone Ranger and Tonto. We used to hurry to see them at the Hippodrome and Strand Theaters on High St. It cost 12 cents to see the movies. Then later on the cost of the movies was raised to 33 cents. Oh yes, about never to miss Bible Class. I wonder. Not so fast, now. She did encourage us to learn all the books of the Bible. Yes, I remember, it was 27 books in the New Testament, and it was 39 books in the Old Testament. I can still remember that! Also, I remember that she taught us many Christian songs. We did enjoy singing together at Bible Class. Those that attended her classes were all from different ethnic groups. She was very fair about that. She showed no partiality, because if she had shown partiality, we would not have continued to go there.

One day a friend, Everline invited me to spend the weekend with her. Her mother and my parents said it would be all right. It was in the summertime. One night, her brother told us, he knew where we could find some good eating apples. We went there and starting picking a few apples. He said it would be okay. All of a sudden a man came outside with a gun and started shooting at us. We ran as fast as we could. I became very angry with him. All of us could have been killed. He didn't tell us the truth. When I recall the incident, I realize how "naive" I was at the time. I assumed that he had permission to pick some of the apples, of course?

Today was a lovely day, and I ran outside to play. My Mother called me to come back in. She said, "Arsonia, you're out here playing and you haven't had your hair combed and brushed." She said, besides you're looking nice, you need to have your hair combed and brushed so that the blood can move about in your head so as to keep your memory intact, so that you'll be able to remember more things. There was a slight problem. I was "tender-headed". You probably wouldn't know what that means, but I'm certain that your hairdresser could tell you what it means. I had very coarse hair, and it tangled easily. My Mother had to take it real easy when she combed and brushed my hair. One day I had enough, and I decided to remove some of the hair from my head. I cut it off and hid it in a bucket. When my Mother realized what I had done, she was quite upset. She scolded me "through tears", and tried to fix my hair. I had some bald spots on my head, so I had to wear a "scull" cap on my head when I went to school until my hair grew back. My teacher asked me what had happened to my hair. I looked at her very "sheepishly", and I told her what I had done. She grinned and shook her head from side to side. I then, of course, realized what I had done, especially after looking in the mirror after I had done it. I never did that again.

I remember those Weekly Readers that we used in school. We gained a lot of knowledge from them, though the leaflets were so very thin. We were all good readers, because we learned to read by Phonetics rather than from memorizing the words. Once you learned the beginning sounds; (b,c,d,f,g,h,j,k,l,m,n,p,q,r,s,t,v,w,x,y,z) well–the vowels (a,e,i,o,u) whether long or short were no problem at all. It was a cinch after that! When we were taught the beginning sounds, and it was our turn to make the sound, you felt as if one's "spit" would consume you. You know what I mean (b-b-b-b-b-b-). Good gracious! It was awful (smile). In any event we learned. We learned mostly because we "shut up" and listened. We knew we had to learn the things that the teacher was teaching us. To tell the truth, it was fun learning. Our teachers, though stern at times, made it a lot of fun. By the way, I had to be able to read. Why? You know? I enjoyed reading the comic books. It was "Flash Gordon", "Superman", "Dagwood and Blondie", "Popeye", "Spiderman", and "Mighty Mouse". We would lie down on the floor of our home and read and read. When we couldn't afford to buy another comic book (They were 10 cents), we would just trade/exchange our books with some of our friends.

Now before we got our report cards in school, there were different colored papers that were sent home with you to give to your parents. No, we didn't throw them away. You'd better not! They didn't play that in our day and time. The colored papers were as follows: A blue slip meant that your work was excellent, a pink slip meant that your work was good, a yellow slip meant that your work was satisfactory, and the white slip–well you know what that meant, don't you? You might now have to stay in the "hot house" (There were no air-conditioners then, either) for a couple of weeks, if you got a white slip. You could get some air from an electric fan if your home had electricity, though. By the way, do you remember when the kids used to run behind the "bug spray" car, soaking up all those fumes blowing on their faces while they chased it? They thought it was so much fun! It's a wonder they're all still alive. "Honest?"

In our family there were four girls. Three of us sang in a Trio. We were called the Glenn Trio. We wore navy-blue "jumpers" with white blouses. We sang around town. I remember that we sang at the Pottstown Public Library, at our local church, Second Baptist Church; and one time we sang at the First Baptist Church. We struggled a "wee" bit, because my oldest sister, Berwindale recently had her tonsils removed. Loretta sang first soprano, Berwindale sang second soprano, and I sang alto. Mrs. Alma Aikens accompanied us on the piano. We got through it okay, I must say.

Every Monday night we would congregate at Bailey and High Streets, here in town, to catch the bus to Ringing Rocks Skating Rink. We paid a reasonable fee for the ride to the rink. We could bring our own roller skates, or we could rent them at the rink. If we brought our own skates, then we paid only to skate. If we didn't bring our own skates, then we paid to rent their skates, and we paid to skate. When I speak about using your own skates, I'm speaking about the roller skates that were built attached to the shoe–not the street skates. The street skates, in those days, were the ones that you put onto your walking shoes. You used a special turn key that was utilized to tighten them onto your regular walking shoes. In addition to the people that came from town to skate there, there were people that came from far away places every Monday night, also.

You need to understand that it was black peoples night. We didn't "hinge" on that, at the time. We were just glad that we were able to come together and enjoy ourselves skating to expend our energy in an enjoyable way. They had a floor for beginners set aside from the floor for the people who knew how to skate well. No one can forget the hot-dogs that they sold there. They were the best tasting hotdogs anywhere in the world. If anyone got out of order, they would escort them to the door. If they refused to leave the premises, the police were called. They did not tolerate any foolishness.

The different versions of skating were as follows: Couples Only, a man and a woman, Trios only–your choice of two men and a woman, or two women and a man–they would announce. Another time they would say, "Clear the floor!" We got off that floor in a hurry.

"The next song to be skated is for men only." "Skate at your own risk!" The men would skate like "crazy!" We also did the "limbo". They lowered a bar to the floor, and you had to skate underneath the stick until it was impossible for you to bend your back any lower under the bar.

The last song skated for the night was for couples only. So they "dimmed" the lights. It was a romantic thing, I suppose. Many times I didn't get to skate the last dance. I didn't care. Finally they would say again, "Clear the floor." "Return your skates." "Goodnight." Finally, we headed for the bus that was waiting outside to pick us up and take us back to Bailey and High Streets. Upon exiting the bus, once in a while a fight would break out. They would let the two fight it out, and then they would break it up so that no one got hurt. Now you heard me say–the two of them fighting. There were no gangs. Then they would say, "Now stop it and go home!" The best thing that happened was that no one got stabbed, shot or was killed. How about that for the "good old days?"

In addition to Monday night skating, our church had Sunday School picnics at the Ringing Rocks Park. They would have "doggie" roasts, and they would roast marshmallows. They would have games such as the potato race. That is, you had to get inside a large brown "burlap" bag (used to hold potatoes), and see who could race to the finish line first. They also had "peanut scrambles". We, too, had hay rides to the park. We had a lot of chaperones. They didn't let you get away with anything, either.

That brings to mind the time I was in school. I was a very talkative child, after graduating from being a very "shy" child. My teacher told me to stop talking so much. Later on I started talking too much again. She said, "Arsonia, hold your hands out in front of me." I held out my hands. She took a ruler and hit me on my fingers because I kept talking. Today that is called "child abuse". In my day it was called, "Now, I guess you'll be quiet now." She was absolutely right! It didn't damage my mind mentally or otherwise. What it did was–stung my fingers and made me be quiet. That's all. Wait until my Mom hears about this. She'll take care of me on my bottom. We were well-behaved kids in those days (child abuse?) You must be kidding?

We played many games on “Chicken Hill”. We played marbles. That’s why the knuckles on my hands look a bit unsightly. I never thought about the fact that someday I would want to have beautiful hands for someone to hold. First you drew a circle in the dirt on the ground. I had a pretty white marble that was called a “troll”. I would use it to shoot my marbles out of the circle, while it “spun” around and remained in the circle. We took turns shooting the marbles out of the circle to see who could win the most marbles. Once your “troll” rolled out, you lost your turn. You’d better not get caught shooting before the line. That was called “gunching”. I remember having badly “skinned up” knuckles from playing marbles. The bruises really burned, and at night we put ointment on our knuckles to help heal our hands. We were a “glutton” for punishment, because no way were we going to stop playing marbles.

Also we had Yo-yo Tournaments. A yo-yo was a colored double two-part circular piece of wood. It had a narrow stick attached in the middle to the double piece of wood. It had a long mobility type string attached to it that wrapped around it. You were to roll the string up and down using your middle finger. It had a loop at the end of the string to fit your middle finger. Some people were able to roll the yo-yo up and down and continue rolling it to the floor. They called this, “walking the dog.” I don’t know why. It was excellent for your hand coordination. We also played “Pick-Up Sticks”. You were to throw the sticks down on a table or the floor and try to pick up each stick, one at a time. You were to do this without touching any of the other sticks and without making any of them move. If any of the sticks moved while you tried to pick one up, you lost your turn. On and on it went. You had to be very skillful with your hands. The person who collected the most sticks won the game. Remember playing with the “Old Maid Cards?” You dealt the cards, but no one knew who had the old maid until luckily someone pulled the card from your hand. This was a serious game. “Whew”. It was like we would become an “Old Maid”. You’d think it was “etched in stone” the way we “fussed and fumed”– as if the cards would make us an “Old Maid” (ha,ha).

There were a lot of areas in town that were not yet developed. There were overgrown lots, fields, junkyards, etc. There were also a number of unpaved streets which created a lot of dust in our homes. We were great tree climbers in those days. It would be no problem for us to select a tree to climb, and then sit out on a tree limb just to talk.

We would enjoy seeing such insects as the ladybug, and we would say, “Ladybug, ladybug, fly away home.” “Your house is on fire and your kids will burn up.” To this day, I don’t know who made up that line. Some of us thought we might turn out to be trapeze artists like in a circus.

Sometimes we would say, “Let’s go up to Mary Louise’s house and clean off the fruit trees in her yard.” We would holler up the alley and say, “Mary Louise, can we come up to your house?” My Mother and her grandmother were very close friends. She would holler back, “Come on up!” Then we would say, “Can we climb up into your trees and eat what we want?” They had peach trees, cherry trees, pear trees–and all. Some people had apricot trees in their yards. We could eat as much as we wanted. Most of the time we would leave her home with a “bellyache”–mostly because we wouldn’t wait until the fruit was really ripe. We were so immature about things like that. We would do it every year. We never learned our lesson.

Then we would play in Mary Louise’s family garages located in the alley way. We would take those old canning jars, put candles in them, and then we would light them and hang them on the walls in the garage. We put old rags around the candles to hold them in place. The Lord certainly took good care of us, because we could have easily started a fire, and all of us could have been burned to death. Imagine that! By the way we caught a cat, put him in a small burlap bag and spanked his “hiney”. We wanted to see what sound he would make when he cried. It hollered "me-ow, me-ow" and wrestled until it freed itself from the bag. We all jumped back and yelled. Then all of us ran to our homes. What did we prove? Absolutely nothing!

Another time Dodge, Sage and I saw a little hole near the floor of the kitchenette of our home. We discovered that a little mouse kept peeking out of its hole. We, three, had a plan. Let's catch it, hold it by the legs, tie a string around his legs and spank him, too, to see what sound he makes. One of my sisters "tattled" on us–ran and got my Mom. My Mom said, "You kids get up from there, don't you know that a mouse is a filthy thing, and that you shouldn't touch it?" Later that evening, my Mother told my Dad, and he set a mouse trap. So much for trying to spank a mouse to see what kind of sound he'd make.

We took very good care of our shoes, too. The shoes that we wore, were made of the finest leather. The only thing that you needed to do when the soles of our shoes wore out, was to get them "re-soled and re-heeled". The reason we could do this is because there was a "shoe man" named "Duggie", that repaired our shoes. You could have them "re-soled and re-heeled" over and over again, and your shoes lasted a long time. That was good because your parents did not have the money to keep buying us new shoes all of the time. They don't make shoes out of that kind of leather today. Also, each child owned two pair of shoes. One for "Sunday go meeting" and one, for everyday, going to school and elsewhere. By the way, we wore white, brown, black or red high-top shoes until we entered first grade. My parents always said we needed to wear them that length of time to properly form our feet and to keep our feet strong. Today it is considered a myth. I don't really know. I remember that they felt good, though. I also remember our wearing those long thick stockings in the winter to keep our legs warm when we no longer wore leggings. Leggings were long wool pants with straps attached to the pants to hold them on. The leggings extended from the hips to the ankles. The leggings had zippers that you opened to get them on. Then you just pulled the zippers down to your feet to close them. I remember wearing them when I was about four years old . I still have the picture showing me wearing my white coat, white leggings and holding my hands in my white muff to keep my hands warm. You don't see those muffs anymore. Ladies used to wear adult size muffs in those days, too.

Men owned one dress hat. That was no problem, because there was a man who owned a store where men could get their hats cleaned and "blocked". I know of no other store now that does that today. Dad always looked good in his "Sunday go meeting" clothes, too. Yes sir-eeh? On the main drag in town, men could always catch a seat there and get a shoe shine from the younger boys who were trying to make two "bits"– you know. The boys built their own shoe shine boxes out of wood. It was built at a perpendicular angle so that a man's foot could be at a perfect position in order for them to shine their shoes. After a man got a good haircut and his shoes shined, he strutted away with a"toothpick" sticking out the corner of his mouth, telling the world how "cool" he was–strutting around like a "peacock". Men struggled with raising their families, but they were very proud men.

We used to make mud pies–you know? You shoveled up some dirt, mixed it with water and "patted" it into a mud cake. No, we didn't eat the mud cakes. We just sat them on a plate–we just pretended. Most of our playing was "pretense". We would pick some peppermint leaves and add it to our demitasse cups of tea that we made. We added a little sugar. We did, however, drink our tea. Sometimes we would sell it for five cents. Five cents went far in those days. You could buy an awful lot of candy for five cents. I remember the pretty very small tea cups, and saucers we used to play "tea party". Kids came and, we had a lot of fun. If no kids came, I pretended that I had guests. I pretended that I was talking with them, and that they were talking to me You know?

We had a lot of street festivals. There was plenty of food. The street was "blocked off" for a long distance, so that no cars could come through. There was plenty of food for everyone to eat. Some of the church members would play instruments. I remember a man playing the large tuba, another man playing the drums, and another playing the piano. Everyone had a great time! There was no fear of anyone committing a crime or anything like that. Well I guess I forgot to tell you. We had no keys to unlock our doors to get into our homes. Doors were never locked to our homes–all night long. Guess what? No one ever came in to steal anything, either. These are the things, I wanted you to know, and that's one of the reasons that I am writing this book. This book could also be called the book of "yester-year, I suppose.

Last week there was a squirrel who would climb down from the big tree in our yard, looking to get some acorns that were in our yard. I was the "spy" that saw him, and decided that I was going to feed him "personally". Everyday I would sit on the back door steps and wait for the squirrel. My brothers kept saying, "You keep trying to feed that squirrel." "Do you think that squirrel is going to be dumb enough to come and take that nut, that you keep holding, out of your hand?" "No way," they said. My Mother chimed in and said, "When Arsonia puts her mind to do something, she does it." After about five days of waiting and coaxing the squirrel to come and take the nut out of my hand– he did just that. Luckily my Mother happened to be watching. She said, "Can you believe that?"

"Arsonia did get that squirrel to come and take that walnut out of her hand." After he took it, though, he hurried up the tree - real fast! "Now, I hope you'll be satisfied," my Mom said.

Unfortunately, there were some prejudices in our town, though. At the Bethany Center in town there was "tap-dancing" and "puppet shows". We made many puppets and had our own shows at the Bethany Center and at home, too. The tap-dancing was held, once a week, by Price Dancing Studios. We, black children, came one night, and the Caucasian children came on a different night. The "puppet shows: were likewise. It seems strange that I can still remember that. Though prejudices were apparent, our parents would not let us fall into the trap of feeling sorry for ourselves, because of our color. They encouraged us to learn as much as we could, and told us, just to try and move on, because there would come a day when it would not be this way.

I was able to let some things go, until it came to music class in Junior High School. There was a song called, "Old Black Joe." Some of the children in the class were amused, but I did not find it funny–not at all. I told my parents about the song, and they told me that when they got to that line–not to sing it. They said that if the teacher had a problem with that, I should let them know. They said that if she became annoyed by it, they would come up to the school and voice their displeasure. I told the teacher what they said, and her face turned "scarlet". I don't remember our having to sing it in music class anymore.

I feel that the fact that we had such nice neighbors, and such a good camaraderie with them, helped us to hold up under the prejudices that we had to face. Mom and Dad did not want us to have any excuses for not learning, but they rather pushed for us to get a good education. They were "sticklers" for wanting us to gain a lot of knowledge. They said "No matter what else happens, you must have a good education." Of course, this was in addition to our spiritual life, which we always had. If you were living, if you were breathing, you went to Sunday School and church every week! This was in addition to going to Mrs. Yergey's Bible Study on Saturdays, and weekly prayer services in our home. On Sunday, you had Sunday School and morning services. In the afternoon, you attended (B.Y.P.U.), Baptist Young Peoples Union, and Sunday night, there were church services again. Early Sunday evenings, the Salvation Army Church Band would congregate at the corner of Beech and Adams Sts. One man blew the trumpet, another played the drums. The rest of them sang hymns, etc. Everyone would be respectful, and would join in with them singing. They stood right in front of our home. Cars came by–one or two every once in a while. When they came at that particular time, they would turn and just go down another street rather than to disturb the services. Sometimes the "Elephant Man" (he was called) would come to Pottstown. I don't know where he "hailed" from. He wore skates on the top part of his legs (I guess his thighs), and he would play his "mandolin". He was able to move about by way of skates. We were a little afraid of him, mostly because he was physically "impaired". No one made fun of him, though. That was the one thing my Mom and Dad would not allow us to do. They would always say, "Don't ever laugh or poke fun at anyone, because the same thing that has happened to them can happen to you or your children, too. I'll never forget that statement as long as I live. I always knew in my heart that they were right.

We played another game. You threw the ball on the outside wall of your home and you would call certain words. You would then throw the ball, touch your knee and quick catch the ball. You would next throw the ball, touch your toe and then quick catch the ball again. Then throw the ball against the wall, quick turn all the way around, and catch the ball without dropping it. You had to be adept in doing this. We also played "kick the can", which was much the same as playing baseball. That is you kicked the can instead of the ball. Were there any accidents? There were just a few minor ones. Also we would crush empty vegetable cans and wear them on the bottom of our shoes and just pranced around with them for fun. I don't remember anyone cutting their feet on the cans. It was a lot of fun! Wow!

There were many playgrounds open all through town. Each playground had a Captain. They would keep order and watch the children to prevent accidents. I remember their giving us so much "gimp" to make key chains and "change purses". The recreation department provided the playgrounds with strips of different colored material. I can't tell you how many "pot holders" we made and took home. The boys, as well as the girls, made the products, too, from the goods donated to the playground. My question is? What happened to the playgrounds that were supervised by the Captains? I guess, all of us know why we can't have them now.

To the back of our property line was a "dump". There were snakes, ticks, rodents, and everything imaginable in that dump. People used to dump even their empty food cans there. It was awful! Beginning in the spring of every year, my Dad would get all of us together to clean up the dump. He started cleaning the dump in 1943. We used a pick, a shovel, a hoe, garden rake, a sickle, and my Dad used the scythe. For those of you who are not familiar with a sickle, it was a curved hook-like blade mounted on a short handle used for cutting unsightly weeds. The scythe, that my Dad used, was a curved blade fastened to a very long handle used for cutting down overgrown grass and weeds. I believe the scythe was as tall as my Dad, and my Dad was a tall man, too! I distinctly remember that. I also remember that my family moved from our first home, at 657 Beech St. to our new home at 631 Beech St. The area in back of our home is where the "dump" was located. They moved there when I was being transported by ambulance back home from the hospital after having my appendix removed. I had acute appendicitis and had been rushed to the hospital prior to their moving there. When they brought me back home, I told them that my family moved up the street. They didn't believe me, and when they were going to take me out of the ambulance, our former neighbors yelled, "Her family moved up the street!" "Don't take her in there!" Her Mom and Dad bought another house. Maybe we could now call "Chicken Hill", "Poultry Heights" "Huh?"

Yes, my Dad and all of us cleaned up the dump until 1963 (for twenty years) and did not receive any enumeration of money from the borough of Pottstown. My Dad didn't care. He also cut down tall trees. He would climb up the trees and start sawing the tops off first. He would then cut the trees lower and lower. Finally he would tie ropes around the trunk of the tree, going in the proper direction. He would continue sawing at the bottom, and then he would pull the rest of the tree down. He did this every year in an effort to clean up the "dump". A man by the name of Mr. Carter would drive his truck around to collect the trash. He was the only trash collector that I knew at the time. He also took away neighbors' discarded ashes from their coal stoves. They each paid him for his services. It was his own private business, and the money that he made, of course, helped to support his family during the post-depression years. A loaf of bread or a dozen of eggs were about 10 cents in those days.

Did anyone tell you the tale about the "headless horseman" and the "ball of fire" that was seen racing through Far Fields where many baseball games were played. That tale was spoken of by many people. I do, however, remember seeing a woman walk straight through the fence at Far Fields (told to us that it was a ghost). When we saw this happen, we raced home– the dust retreating right behind us!

One day a "Ho-Bo" came to our house. My Dad allowed him to come in. We couldn't believe it! My Dad asked my Mother to give him a plate of food. We had a kitchen that we ate in and a kitchenette that my Mother prepared her food in. My Dad sat the "Ho-Bo" in a chair as my Mother was giving him some food. We were all "peering" through the kitchen window to the kitchenette–the windows adorned with pretty white Swiss dotted curtains. My Dad made us get away from the window. The "Ho-Bo" used his hands and "lapsed" up all his food so very fast. We couldn't believe it!

When the man finished eating, my Dad requested my Mother to give him some food that he could take along with him wherever he was going. My Dad also gave him some change and clothing to take with him. My Mom and Dad were good Samaritans. They always chose to help people. It was their way. After the man left, my Dad requested my Mother to throw the plate away. Every once in a while another one would appear. It was said that "Ho-Bo's" leave clues for others, to let them know who will feed them. They say that they place a stone on a wall or whatever in plain view for another "Ho-Bo" to see. Yes, my Mom and Dad fed many people, but I have to say that we were blessed to have them for our parents. At times, my Dad worked two jobs to provide for our care. He would not take any charity.

Each year before our school closing, we celebrated our "May Pole Day". A beautiful May Pole was erected in the center of the school playground. We also selected a May Queen who would be dressed as such. Each classroom, from first to sixth grade would perform, one after the other, until all classes gave their performance. I remember the year that we did the

"Indian Dance". I can still remember the tune. We would put our right hand to our forehead and then our left hand to our forehead while we were doing a classic Indian step. We did this while we were turning our bodies to the right, and then turning our bodies to the left. We approached it as if it were the performance of our lives. After all performances were completed, different performers would grab hold to one of the colorful streamers on the May Pole and go around in different directions, while the music played. The streamers remained "untangled" the whole time, because of the way that the pole was constructed, I suppose. May Day was our most favorite day.

However, let's not forget about the festivals at Jefferson School, too. The teachers and volunteers would prepare all the food inside the school, open up the windows and sell you the food while you waited by the outside windows. They had clowns, too. We ate candy, popcorn, candy cotton, peanuts (5 cents a bag) and all. They sold delicious hot-dogs in those days (pure beef) hot dogs (10 cents). I never had a hot dog that tasted like the hot dogs that we ate at the school festivals. All of our teachers were in attendance there. They took that opportunity to see your parents and to let them know how things were going with their children. Your behavior was an essential part of your school life. Mom always said, "I'm not sending you to school to behave like a monkey!" "I'm sending you to school to learn." "If you feel that you can't learn anything, at least you ought to be able to behave yourself." "There's nothing "cute" about being "bad", she would always say.

Another activity that we enjoyed was when we made our own "bows and arrows". We would cut a certain type branch off of a tree. We would peel off the covering of the branch until we could see the white milk from under the covering. We would then wipe it dry. Later we would take a sharp knife and peel off all the bumps from the stick that we selected. We would carve the stick until it became very smooth and flexible. Then we would cut a "slit" into each end of the "bow". Next, we would select some "shoots" from certain kinds of trees, shape them, and then we would use them as arrows. We made the best "bows and arrows" in Pottstown!

The local movie theaters raised their movie prices from 12 to 33 cents. I was not happy about that; therefore, I decided to make my own movies. I got a cardboard box that was opened in the front. I made two round holes in each side of the box. Then I got my Mom's rolling pin that she used to roll out her dough when she made pies and /or dumplings. I placed it, lying it in the areas where I made the two holes. I retrieved magazines and cut out all kinds of pictures and pasted them together and rolled them around the "rolling pin" to represent a film. Then I held a flashlight behind the pictures to represent a camera to the movie screen. We turned off the kitchen lights. I used two volunteers to turn the "rolling pin" around and around until all the pictures were seen. My sisters complained, because one minute, you would see a man, then the next minute you would see a can of baked beans. Next, you may see a car, then maybe, you would see a dog. Nothing matched up at all. Well, so what" You only paid a nickel to get in, you know. I charged each person a nickel to see the "homemade" movies. At intermission, one of my brothers, Dodge and I danced. Once he threw me in the air, and I landed on the floor. Everyone laughed hysterically. I didn't get hurt, though. I laughed, too. Well, every movie has to have some entertainment at intermission, don't they? Anyway, we had a great time, and I made "me" some good money!

This part of the story tells about some unusual circumstances that happened to me to which I can't fully understand. I was nine years of age at the time. I had awaken in the middle of the night, because I felt as though something was "tugging" me. I quickly opened up my eyes, and I saw such a bright, bright light! It appeared to enter through the bedroom window– late at night I recall. I tried so very hard to look at it, but it was too bright! I pulled up my blanket to shield me from this magnificent light. I felt I needed to look again, but somehow I felt I dare not do it. I screamed for my Mother, but she did not respond. Eventually I lapsed into a deep sleep. The next day, I went into my parent's bedroom to talk to my Mother. She inquired of me as to why I was so "hoarse". I told her what happened and the fact that I called for her help. She said that I must have been dreaming. What I was envisaging last night was much too difficult to explain to anyone, so I just let it go. I never, never forgot, though.

Sometime later on, I became enlightened to a fact that is written in the Bible that I had not previously known or had never been told. It is in the book of Exodus, Chapter 33, Verse 20 which says and I quote: “And he said, Thou canst not see my face: for there shall no man see me, and live.” That solved the mystery for me, and it solved it real well. I think of that encounter every once in a while, because I didn’t know why it happened. Later on I had an aura type meeting with I believed to be the appearance of Satan, not gruesome looking as I had expected, but it left me with a real “eerie” feeling. Shortly after those two encounters, I accepted Jesus Christ as my Savior (a group of us), and I was baptized, at aged 9 by the late Reverend Heywood L. Butler whom I dearly loved. It came to my remembrance that I took two pennies from a neighbor’s table to buy two balloons at Brunish’s grocery store. After I was baptized, I ran back down the street from where I took the pennies and put them back on the table without saying a mumbling word. It was something that I felt that I had to do, and I felt so much better after I had done it.

Tuesday mornings was the day that I went down to clean my Uncle “Fathead’s” home. As I entered his parlor, I found him speaking to “angels”. I heard him say, Angels go away, and he was pushing them away, although I didn’t see them, myself. It made me terribly upset, as you can understand. I felt, in my own heart, that this was not a good sign–not at all. I told no one. My Uncle, my son, “Bugsy” and I always ate breakfast with him every Tuesday morning. We looked forward to this every week. My husband was at work and my daughter, Lannette, was at school, but I did not work at the time, because “Bugsy” was only three years old. When I finished cleaning his home, he handed me his laundry, as he always had done. However, this time he told me to take his laundry back home with me, because he wouldn’t be needing it anymore. I returned home later and told my Mother what he said. She said, “Just keep it for now, don’t upset him, and then just take them back with you, because he’ll ask for it again, I’m sure.” It was a nice Fall day in October, and this was the day we were due to go down and clean my Uncle “Fathead’s” home again. When I got three blocks from my home it started to rain. (I didn’t drive at the time.) My son always walked with me, so I decided to turn around and return instead on Wednesday. A little later, the sun came back out, so I decided to try it again. As soon as I got about three blocks away, it again started to rain. Finally, we turned back, and I decided I would not try it again today. this going back and forth was wasting my day, and going down another day would not matter at all. It really upset me, because, as I said before, he would serve my three year-old son and me breakfast. We, three, would eat together on that day. We looked forward to that every week, because he was very special to me. Whatever my parents weren't able to give me, my Uncle "Fathead" would. One year he gave me some additional money to buy me a beautiful gray suit for Easter.

In finishing the story, I must tell you that had it not been for the drizzles and the rain, I would have made it down to my Uncle's home, and I would have discovered his dead body–my little son and I. Apparently, he had collapsed at his home and died. If I had made it to his home and found him dead, I most likely would have had a "heart attack", because he meant the world to me. To have had my young son with me would have been a total disaster. I feel that the good Lord protected me by sending the drizzle and rain each time I tried to get closer to his home. In my heart, I truly believe this is why it happened in this way. My Uncle was definitely right, just like he said. He told me he wouldn't be needing his laundry that I had laundered for him anymore. He certainly was right! His laundry was home with me. He wanted me to have it. He didn't need them anymore. He was right. Can you imagine that! I guess the "death angels" came back to get him, and this time he finally surrendered and went with them, because now he was ready. He was later found dead by two of his nephews.

Premonitions and visions have been a recurrent part of my life. Some extra-sensory perceptions have taken hold of me at times. I saw one of my two sons in a casket in a "vision" one night. I pulled at the handkerchief covering my child's face to see which one I would lose, but broke out in a "cold" sweat and immediately woke up. I then knew that I would lose one of them. I lost my youngest child in the prime of his life to cancer. Can you believe that! I saw my Father's face pass in front of me less than ten minutes before he passed. It really shook me!

My Father and I had delivered Christmas presents the night before, out in the country to some of his friends. That was the last time we were together. It really shook me! It really did! Wow!

We used to play croquet at my Uncle "Fathead's" home. It was an outdoor game that you played by knocking wooden balls through a series of iron arches by means of mallets. In this game, the act of driving away an opponent's ball by striking one's own when the two are in contact. This was quite an enjoyable game. It was so much fun. We also played horse-shoes. That was a game using horse-shoes or similar pieces,–the object being to throw the piece so as to encircle an iron stake 30 or 40 feet away. The men would get "wild" playing this game. They just loved it.

Besides this, my Uncle maintained a vegetable garden. You could bet on taking some delicious vegetables along home. He also had a lot of grapevines. We used to pick grapes to make grape jelly. He also had mulberries–some white ones and some red, black or reddish-purple mulberries. You hardly see or hear of mulberries today. Then, too, he had some raspberries in his yard. Some were black, some purple. The thing about raspberries was that you had to be careful, because snakes hung around those berries all of the time. Many times we found ourselves "spooked" away from a raspberry bush because a snake was "lurking" there. Once I dropped my whole box of berries, and I made a mad dash out of the bushes. I never liked a snake–never!

Every year we would have New Year's Dinner at Uncle "Fathead's" home. They just loved that, because he would not let us reprimand the children. He would always say, "Let the children alone." "You know you were a child once, yourself". "They have to learn." We would stare at our children to let them know that they still had to go home with us. However, he would give all the children goodies on that day. He would give them oranges, apples, candy canes, nuts, etc. He would cook a full course turkey dinner with all the "trimmings". He would also have duck, ham and pheasant for us to eat. It was a splendid meal! All of us remember those days with Uncle "Fathead", I can tell you that. He's the only one that would have a whole coconut for us to enjoy. We just loved that! I loved chewing the coconut that he gave us.

During one winter month, Sage and some of the others, including me, decided to go sledding down the hill connected to our yard. It was actually our neighbor's yard (the Jackson's) that had a good incline for sledding. Sage was to steer the sled, and the rest of us all jumped on. We came rushing down the hill at quite a fast pace. Sage lost control of his steering and hit the "bucket-a-day" coal stove that was sitting in our yard–and all of us fell off the sled. The sad part about it was that Sage lost his front teeth in the ordeal. He didn't get them replaced until he went into the U. S. Army. We often teased him about the sled ride. Speaking of teeth, all of us went to the school dentist. Our parents only had to pay 50 cents for a dentist visit. However, in those days, you either got your tooth "filled" or "pulled".

That's it! When the dentist would drill a hole into your tooth to clean out the cavity, he would pour "cold water" into that tooth to rinse out the particles with its "zillions" of nerves sitting there in your mouth to "electrocute" you. They didn't have enough common sense to use warm water like the dentists do now. That's why so many people told the dentist to just pull it out and get it over with. "Root Canal?" You must be kidding!!!

We performed Operettas at the Bethany Center. We danced around and sang on a stage at the center. We wore crepe paper outfits that the ladies made for all the performers. In fact, crepe paper was used for church plays in those days, too. You'd be surprised to see how nice the outfits were that we wore; and they were quite colorful, also. The crepe paper was a thin paper that looked wrinkled to resemble crepe, a type of cloth. You could twist the paper in any direction, and oftentimes they sewed parts of it together to look like a special wearing apparel in order to look like a certain type character in the operetta. Mrs. Martin was our choral director.

Also in the lower area of the center was a mechanical horse track. By that I mean, they had metal horses that we would pedal. Each horse had two pedals, one on the right side of the horse, and one on the left side of the horse. Everyone would grab an empty horse, when no one was riding it, and all would pedal as fast as they could. The horses went around and around similar to a carousel. We would get it up to top speeds. It was a wonderful invention. I wonder whatever happened to it. I've never seen even a close resemblance of that mechanical horse track that they had at Bethany Center. This track was stationed on the floor, whereas with a carousel it sits up high on a platform, and the horses are much larger than what these were. These were much more fun, because we ran those mechanical horses at a high rate of speed until the Director of the Center, Mr. Dick Ricketts, would catch us and make us slow down. Wow! What a ride! That was fun; It really was a lot of fun pedaling those horses around the track!

I think back at the time we got our shots from the doctor. Everyone that wasn't getting a shot said, "Now don't holler!" "Now don't yell!" Also when they gave you a good spanking, they would say, "Now you better not cry." What I want to know is who came up with that metaphor? Of course, you're going to holler. Of course, you're going to cry. Remember when they used to spank us and say, "You know this hurts me more than it hurts you." I didn't know what in the world they were talking about then. "Okay, I know now."

Remember when we used to play with our paper dolls. They were cut out of cardboard–boys and girl dolls. We would cut out different outfits from the books, and put the paper dresses on the dolls. They had little tabs on the paper outfits that you just folded around the top, middle and lower parts of the dolls, and then you would just lay them down. If you've never seen them, then you wouldn't have any idea of what I'm talking about. However, I just loved cutting out all the different changes of clothing and putting them on my paper dolls. This was a project usually for girls.

One of my neighbor's little baby was "fussy" today. I heard her say that she was going to prepare some catnip tea for the baby. Catnip tea was a plant of the mint family with strongly scented leaves of which cats are fond. When they gave it to their babies, apparently, it calmed them down. You rarely hear about it nowadays. One day my Dad was "shucking corn", and I had an idea. I decided to take the brown dry part, below the silk portion of the corn, to use it to put hair on my doll. I retrieved it and pasted some on the top of my doll's head. The rest I put into braids and attached it onto the rest of the hair on her head. I know it's hard to believe, but it worked out real well, and my doll was no longer bald-headed. Some of my friends were certain that I would see worms appear in the hair, but no worms "showed up". I assume it was because the silk from the corn was now brown and very dry.

A couple of us in the family had a bad cold. My Dad had a remedy that the doctors couldn't believe when I told them how he got rid of our colds. He would mix just a little coal oil (i.e., kerosene), turpentine and sugar together. Then using an eyedropper, he would squeeze a couple drops down our throats. I know that's hard to believe, and I wouldn't dare do it now; however, that's how he cured a "cold" back then. We laugh about it all the time, but we didn't die–now did we?

My brothers had a way of making some money, but it was not easy. They did some caddying for men at the country club. They would get a few of their friends together and would take some sleeping gear with them to sleep in the "caddie shack" at the golf course. They wanted to be the first ones to get to carry the golf bags (no carts in those days). They also learned how to dispense the golf clubs for the golfer after doing it over a period of time. All of them learned how to do it. They told me that they would get some cat o' nine tails and light them to keep the mosquitoes away. They would also take some snacks along with them, too, for when they got hungry. Apparently it was decent money, because they did this every weekend when they were out of school.

Did you hear about the "out house"? Oh, you don't know what an "out house" is? Why was it called an "out house"? It was called an "out house", because you had to go outside to use it. It was the place to go to eliminate the wastes from your body. I know, I know, but that's the way it was. That's all I can tell you. One day we saw a lady enter our "out house". We never saw her come out. We summoned my Mother to tell her. She waited with us. My Mom said, "Are you certain that you saw a woman go in there?" "All three of us saw her, Mom" Finally, my Mom opened the door and saw no one. An investigation was ensued by my Dad. The final assumption was that it was a ghost, and that we should just let it be. So, we just let it be. However, we used to talk about it whenever we reflected back on the "good old days"–if that's what you want to call it. It was "dubious"–good and bad.

Mr. Powell wrung a chicken's neck and killed it to have for his supper. After it stopped "flopping" around and was declared dead, he had to start cleaning it. He dipped the chicken into some hot boiling water to wet the feathers to make it easy to pull off the feathers. Prior to that he had made a little fire outside. Then he just kind of ran the body of the chicken over the lit fire to burn off the small pieces of hair from underneath the feathers. He put out the fire, and he finished cleaning the chicken, and continued picking the needles off of the chicken's skin. Now you know what came next?

You guessed it! He "gutted" out the chicken after he placed a lot of newspapers under it on his "workers bench". He picked all the chicken "guts" up and discarded them. How did he discard them? He dug a nice size whole in the ground and just buried them. He buried them deep enough, so that it wouldn't draw any flies, I was told. He did not, however discard the heart, the liver, feet or gizzard. Oh yes, some people in those days "sucked" some of the juice out of chicken feet. "Oooooh!" "No way!" All of that was "edible". I'm not finished. Lastly, he dipped the chicken in cold water, a number of times to clean it up real nice. He soaked it in an oblong pail and gave it a real good washing. It came out real clean. It really did! Now don't you go giving Mr. Powell a bad name. Pardon my "colloquialism", but this way of killing chickens, etc. went on long before Mr. Powell. What about the Pilgrims with their turkeys in Rhode Island and all. Also, you know the story about John Smith, the founder of Jamestown, Virginia enjoying their fowl dinners. They probably learned it from the American Indians, I am sure.

Probably one of those Indians accidentally dropped a couple pieces of dry corn in the cooking oil and "low and behold" (serendipity) occurred and popcorn was born. Accidentally, many things happen "out of chance", you know.

I remember an incident that occurred in high school. We were returning back to our class when all of a sudden the students sat me down in the wastepaper can. I was very "skinny" in those days, so I fit the can quite well. Then the teacher arrived behind us and saw me in the wastepaper can. She said, "Now who put Arsonia in the wastepaper can?" Everyone by then had quickly ran and sat in their seats. No one uttered a single word. Then she asked me who put me in the wastepaper can. I said, "They just put me in here, teacher." She then put her hands on her hips and said, "All of you–get up here and get Arsonia out of the wastepaper can!" The class knew that they were bound for "detention"!

The girls pulled my legs out. The boys grabbed me by my long "slinky" arms and helped me out. Then we all ran to our seats. We thought we would be in big trouble for sure–not me though. Finally our teacher frowned at all of us and said, "Now that's ridiculous to do that to Arsonia!" I tried to look real pitiful, so I wouldn't get my class in trouble. I was always a "good sport". I wasn't angry at all. Then all of a sudden, the teacher "burst" out and laughed. We all laughed, too. She then said, "Don't you dare let this ever happen again, you hear me?" They all chimed in, "No, ma'am, we won't." After school, all of us laughed about it. They meant no harm to me. I knew that.

This is a story about how people survived after the 1929 Depression. There is some nostalgia given in the daily newspapers from time to time about things that happened in the past. However, I wanted to tell you my side of the story as I remembered it, from the time that I was at least four years old. I call this story, "The Legend of Chicken Hill."

Sometimes when we ran out of toothpaste, we used baking soda or salt to brush our teeth, and also gargled with it to clean our breath until mouth wash finally arrived. Today some toothpaste have now included baking soda as an added ingredient. Imagine that!

One day I burned my hand on the kitchen stove. My grandfather, who came to visit us, was in the house at the time. He took my hand, blew at my hand, and prayed a prayer. After he finished praying he said, "Now daughter, how does your hand feel now?" It didn't hurt anymore, at all. I couldn't even see where I had burned it. It really scared me. My grandfather laughed and said that it was okay for me to be astonished about what had just occurred. I marveled at the fact that my grandfather's prayer worked that fast. I just could not get over that. I spoke to others about it years after his passing.

Another thing, too, that he did, was that he baked a cake one day. I told everyone not to jump in the kitchen while his cake was in the oven. He said, "Daughter, come here a minute." "I want you to jump up and down." "My cake will not fall." I did as he had requested me to do. I jumped up and down, and his cake did not fall. I shook my head in amazement!

Our ice box had no more room to store anymore food, and my grandfather had just cooked some vegetables. He said, "I'll just sit the pot "down low" and it will be all right." I said, "Oh no, grandpa, your food will "spoil". He said, "Now you just wait until morning, and you'll see by setting the pot down low that my food will not spoil." In the morning, all of us checked to see if the vegetables "bubbled" to a "spoil". It had not "spoiled". He heated his vegetables and ate some of it to prove to us that the food was fine. We waited to see if grandpa would get sick. Grandpa was fine. If only we would have written down some of these things that we saw grandpa do, we would have gained an insurmountable knowledge of food preparation. That is something I truly regret now. Not only was he a chef, but he was a devout Christian man that we dearly loved.

Someone's baby was again "fussy", and a relative told the parent to give the baby a couple warm drops of nitre. I remember the word vividly. I don't know what was in the liquid, but it worked. It did the "trick".

Did you ever hear of a "Pow Wow" lady. I heard of one who was called "Grammy." The story goes that she was born with a veil over her face, and that she had some strange powers. One day a man who had some medical problems and who was partially crippled decided to give "Grammy" a chance to heal his body. He visited her for about three weeks. She did not accept any money, either. Finally he was healed and no longer crippled. People prefer not to get involved with this type of "holistic" treatment, for fear of the unknown. Though today, of course, it's not recommended. However, a man was healed. In that particular event someone gained something that they had lost. I would be the last one to question such an act at this point, especially since it did not pertain to me. In that respect, I'll just let that be. It is not mine to question. It may have been his faith, for real?

I was told that before I was even born, my sister Berwindale had a very bad cold. Apparently my parents were waiting for the doctor to arrive to help their baby who appeared to be in distress as far as her breathing was concerned. My Mother was really "shook-up". I imagine it was because, her first born child after seven years of wanting to have a child, was born "stillbirth". It seemingly was taking much too long for the doctor to arrive, so this is what my Mother told me that my Dad had done.

He held my sister in his arms and took his mouth and "sucked" out the nasal secretions out of her nose and then, each time, "spit" it out. He did this until he could see that his daughter was able to breath. When the doctor arrived, my Dad told him what he had done. The doctor said that my Father saved my sister's life. How many fathers would have thought to do that for their child. I imagine that he felt that he had no other alternative; therefore, he did that in a state of sheer "panic", I am sure. He had to do some real fast thinking, I suppose. Many years later, they told all of us about the story. Most importantly it all worked out real well.

I used to have terrible "ear aches". My Mother would warm up something called "sweet oil" and put the warm oil in my ears. Sometimes she would blow some cigarette smoke in my ears to help with the pain. There was no known medicine available to cure "ear aches"–what a terrible pain! As a result of this ineffectiveness, I suffered a hearing loss in both of my ears. There were no antibiotics at that time, unfortunately for me. I struggled learning in school, because I had this hearing deficit. There was a strange thing that happened to me, though, one day. A hard piece of something fell out of my one ear. I retrieved it, picked it up and monitored it very closely. I could not "for the life of me" determine how anything like that would have even fallen out of my ear, if it didn't belong there. It resembled a bone. I wrapped it up, very quickly, and put it into a clean handkerchief, placed it in my pocket, and carried it home. I ran upstairs, past my Mother, to my bedroom that I shared with my two sisters. I got out my hygiene book to see what the different parts of the ear, inside, looked like.

I said to myself, "It doesn't look like any of the parts of the inside of the ear that's in my hygiene book." I checked it out for a few days wondering what it was. I was too terrified to tell anyone–even my Mother. I don't know why. It looked bony, gray in color, long and thin. Finally I decided to just bury it in the ground. Later, I worried that I should have kept it. I did not know whether or not it was something that needed to be put back in my ear. It was too late, after I had buried it in the ground, to find that out now.

In our time, we did not use the "F" word. The words we used to call people names were as follows: onion head, cabbage head, googgle eyes, chicken-but nose, boogie, snot, worm, snake, "teacher's brownie", "teacher's pet", tattle-tale, cry-baby, snaggle tooth, pickle face, skinny Minnie, fat rat, fat pig, cream puff and turd. That's as bad as it could get. We weren't perfect, but this was the extent of our name-calling compared to the language that the children use today, and I wanted to share those words with you in my story.

In those days, when you got a real bad cold, they would do one of the following things. If you had a fever, they would take a cheesecloth and fill it with onions and would bind it to your chest. This mixture was used to draw all of the fever out of your body when you had a fever. What our parents did was to plaster your chest with Vicks salve or with a type of mustard paste that they could find and cover your chest with the cheesecloth. After removing it from you in the morning, you had to contend with that smell on your chest for the duration of the cold, because they would not dare open your pores, by washing off your chest in the morning. They would just put layers of clothing on you. They did this, they thought, to keep you from catching pneumonia. They "bundled you up" to save your life they thought.

Well, I'm just telling you what they did. This was their way in those times. Their "main concern", so to speak, was to keep their children alive and well. Their children meant the world to them, in those days. I can't forget those wonderful pillows that were stuffed with "goose feathers"–as was the mattresses. I can't forget the springs that the mattresses sat on. We used to jump up and down on the bed. What a ride! I remember when Mom had church meetings at the house. There were heat vents throughout the house–the heat was circulated throughout the house through the benefit of coal (no gas, oil, or electrical heat) you know. I don't know if it was anthracite or bituminous coal–didn't matter. We had to be in bed when the church members came to the house. Children could not be around in the presence of grown folk when they were talking (gossiping), or whatever. "This just was not allowed, unless you wanted to carry "two lips" on your face. We would lie on the floor, and using a straw, blow peas down the heat vents at the people, and they would jump not knowing what we had done. My Mom excused herself and came upstairs, knowing full well what was going on. She promised us a spanking if we didn't stop immediately! Oh well, it was fun while it lasted. It was!

You might say we were ornery, sometimes, as kids. Therefore, our parents had to discipline us. We knew we were wrong. We always got caught. That was the extent of our bad behavior. We never really did any harm to anyone–we never did–"cross my heart and hope to die". My brothers and some of our neighbors used to do the "hambone". It was a type of clicking their hands throughout their bodies while they made up words and tunes while keeping up with the beat. It was "slap" "clickety-click", "slap", "clickety-click". You couldn't do the "hambone" unless you wore jeans, because wearing the jeans created a certain sound effect that was a significant correlation to the slap from your chest down to your jeans moving your hand and wrist to the beat, which created a certain sound effect. I remember one friend, Jimmy, in particular that was unique in his expression of doing the "hambone". We, girls, were doing the "Charleston". It was a favorite dance of the "gay nineties", we were told. Our parents didn't mind, because it was a clean dance. It was more like a type of exercise, because when you finished doing the "Charleston", you were dead tired. Your feet and legs did the most work even though there was a lot of arm swinging. You had to do a lot of "shuffling" your feet and legs to the rhythm. It was a lot of fun! The boys did the "hambone", and we did the "Charleston". I'm sure you've seen or heard about it. Some of the old folk did it, too. It was good clean fun. It really was. Wow!

We had a friend whose family was really struggling. When they ran out of toothpaste, baking soda, salt or whatever, they brushed their teeth with a bar of soap. Imagine that!

The only time I had soap put in my mouth was when my Mother heard me talking under my breath, because I didn't like something that she wanted me to do. Maybe I said to someone, "Oh my God!"–instead of Oh my goodness!" Or maybe she heard me say to someone, "What in the heck are you talking about?" "Heck" was a curse word. When you said anything like that they washed your mouth out with soap. I should have said, "What in the world are you talking about?" That's the way it was whether we liked it or not. That wasn't child abuse, either. It was "shut up" and clean up your mouth or else!

One of my brothers was disobedient. The bad thing about it was that we lived near a "weeping willow" tree. My Mother told my brother to go outside and bring her a "switch". You may not have heard that word used, but it is in Webster's Dictionary. My brother brought her a small "switch" for her to spank him. He should have known that wasn't going to work. She broke it in half and said, "Now go out there and get me a real 'switch'". He knew exactly what she meant–a bigger one. She then said, maybe you better bring me two of them. Wow!

He then brought her a bigger "switch"–two of them as asked–to my Mother. She took them and braided them together. Uh-oh? We knew what was coming. She said, "Now you come here." She then spanked him and said, "This is hurting me more than it's hurting you, boy." Well at least my brother learned how to tap-dance; because when she "swatted" his legs, he jumped up and down and all around, for just a little bit. She loved her son, but he needed to be disciplined for the changing and cruel world. He was okay with it though. He knew what he did wrong and accepted his punishment quite well.

Now I must tell you about my other brother, Dodge. My Dad caught him smoking a cigarette, and he had warned us not to let him catch us smoking while we were living under his roof. We knew the rules. So, he gave one of the family members some money, and he told them to bring back a couple packs of cigarettes. I said, "Oh no!" "Woe!" When the cigarettes were brought back from the store and given to my Father, let me tell you what he did. He said, "Okay, so you want to be a man, start smoking!" My father lit one cigarette after another and gave it to my brother to smoke. He looked as if he was "turning green".

We finally begged our Dad to not make him smoke anymore cigarettes. He said, "Now do you want to smoke anymore cigarettes in my home?" My brother never said a mumbling word. His lips were sealed! We could tell Dad felt bad about doing it, but he made his point! Guess what? My brother never smoked cigarettes to this very day. How's that for curing a problem before it became an "addiction." Guess what? I never took up smoking, either, after I saw all that (smile.) All of us laugh about it now, but at least we don't have to waste any money, or damage our lungs by buying and smoking cigarettes. How about that!

I must tell you about when Sage got drafted into the U. S. Army. He had passed his physical exam and was told to get down to the train station with his "duffel bag", etc. to take him where he would be stationed. My Dad was busy doing some repair work on the house, the day that Sage was supposed to leave for the Army.

Sage said, "Dad I'm getting ready to go to the train station, leaving for the Army now." My father was not a "huggy-type" person. He was more like a "handshake" or "tipping" his hat type of a person. He turned to my brother, Sage, and said, "Well take good care of yourself, son." My brother told this story, I believe, a hundred times. He said he had to carry his large duffel bag all the way down to the train station. We had no car at home, then. He said that, when he told the service men the story, they laughed and laughed. He said, though, that the strict upbringing and hard work that they had to do at home–cutting up wood and all, paid off. Serving in the Army did not present any problem to him at all. He said the chores in the service were no problem, because of the family discipline and training mandated in our home. One day he shared this story with my Father. My Father laughed, because both of them were much older, and could talk about it then. My Dad laughed and said, "Did I do that son?" "I'm sorry." "I had so many responsibilities at the time, and I didn't realize that I hadn't properly connected with you when you left for the service." My brother, Sage said, "That's okay, Dad." Then they both laughed and laughed. My mother joined in and laughed, too. We laughed until our stomachs hurt. Later they would catch up to my Dad and tease him about that story every once in a while when we began to reminisce. Recalling past experiences, always, was a lot of fun.

Also Sage had been active in sports in school. At Pottstown High, he earned fifteen (15) varsity letters for his performance as a football halfback, baseball, centerfielder, 100- yard and 220 yard runner for the Track team, and as a basketball player. I suppose that added to his capabilities of performing his services in the Armed Forces, also. All of my brothers, in future years played either basketball, football, or track. I must tell you about my brother, Dodge. He was so funny. He would tell us over a hundred times what he had to memorize in Science Class. He said that his Science teacher, named Mr. Wisner, taught him that Science is a body of knowledge that was tested, verified, arranged and classified. I believe he stated this to me a "hundred times". He was a "book worm" much like myself, and he also was a gifted musician. All of our family members played musical instruments such as: piano, organ, drums, marimba, guitar, cymbals, violin, and one took voice lessons much later.

The boys on the block also had a band. They would play right outside on the pavement, while everyone listened to them. They would all get together and perform, and they were really good! Opportunities did not present itself at that time; unfortunately, for they could have gone far with their talents. Different ones that played in the band got drafted into the services while others decided to join the services. This left a void and later left a loss of interest in the continuance of the band. With all of these life changes, the band was unable to hold on.

Dodge, one of the members of the band who volunteered to join the Armed Services, however, played in the United States Air Force Band during his military career. Also, another member of the band, Herman Curtis, went into the Services. When they both left, the band folded and became defunct. They both played professionally in the U.S.–Herman played abroad for a period of time.

I would be amiss if I did not tell you some things that happened with respect to death, etc. in the early years. There were some real "uncanny" things that happened. I don't know the ideology for it either. When school let out, we used to "fly" down the street (figuratively speaking) to see if a funeral wreath was placed on our front door. Upon seeing this on our front door would have meant that someone in the family had died. When a family member lost a loved one in those days, we were not allowed to make any noise, play any games, or even play outside while the family was in "mourning". Also the body was brought to the house for the "wake", and placed in the parlor. People sang hymns and gave prayers over the deceased person. The body remained there until the mortician picked up the body and took it to the church for the funeral services. In other words, I'm telling you that the body remained in the home all night long before the funeral. I can remember having very bad "nightmares" after the death of someone as a child. However, after learning more about God's plan for us, etc. I gained a better perspective and was taught that one's death was not the end if one was properly prepared with the doctrine of Christ in their lifetime. However, the fear remained with me until my adulthood. I was certainly relieved when that fear finally released me.

Nowadays, people do not respect the dead. They destroy markings on the graves and tombstones. I think this is horrible and should be listed as a Federal crime. Once we attended a funeral of a relative and we were having the final rites at a cemetery in a certain city. A young boy raced into the cemetery trying to elude the police. The police had their pistols drawn. I could barely concentrate on the "Lord's Prayer", because I was thinking what if a bullet hits one of us. When the services were over, we said, "What is this world coming to?" "You can't even bury your dead in peace anymore, because crime is prevalent everywhere!"

Since it was a nice summer day, the boys decided to bring their pallets, blankets and pillows outside to sleep on the ground. It was "pitch" dark, but that's what they liked, because they could see all the "going-on's" outside. They had snacks, sodas, etc. Sometimes they would witness domestic quarrels, and they would say, "Hush, let's watch and see what happens." Some of the rest of us would be getting back from the movies, or elsewhere, and they would tell us to hurry into the house so that they could see better. We could hurry into the house, because, in our day and time, we locked no doors. There was no such thing that you needed a key to the door to get in. The doors to our home, as well as our neighbors' homes were never locked, and no one stole anything the entire time that we lived there. Now compare that to these modern times. I admit there's good and bad about the so-called "good old days".

However, we must admit that there's some good and bad about these modern days, too. The most important ingredient that's missing today is the love towards one another. I imagine that's because some of us are depressed people, because of circumstances not under our control, which caused us to become greedy and (self) ish, (self) centered and all the other prefixes of being one's self which is listed in Websters Dictionary. We haven't been willing to make the "switch", so to speak; and therefore, it continues to hold us back. Farther along we will be able to understand and hopefully grow away from the things that keep us pulling one another down.

We were getting ready to leave home to go to school and we heard, "Rrrrrr!–rrrrring!"

The school bell is ringing, and we'd better hurry before we're late. We would go to school, but we would jump rope, singular or "double-Dutch to the very last minute. Others were playing kick-ball, catch-the-ball, and some were shooting marbles. The school bell ringing was to let you know that you needed to get to school. Each week a student was selected to ring the large hand bell. When the second bell sounded, you needed to quickly get inside the building or you were declared, "late for school".

Looking back I remember how many times I took an apple from Mom's house. I would rub it over and over again on my little dress to make it shine. Then, I would take it to school and put it on the front of my teacher's desk. Another day, I would hurry to school to open the door for the teacher. We would argue over who was going to open the door for the teacher. Imagine that! When we went to school, teachers were treated as royalty. They really were! I remember trying to copy the traits of one of my female teachers. I picked up a lot of her mannerisms, because I admired her. Thinking back I now realize how careful one needs to be, because, it is true that children pretend to be others by copying or portraying things that they saw the teachers do. I know that from my own past experiences. Too, I begged the teacher to let me stay after school to wash off the blackboards. It was a job of great honor (smile). When I got to high school, I was allowed to pick up my teacher's tray of food from the cafeteria because of my good behavior (smile). Later, I was called the "teacher's pet"–sometimes they called me the "teacher's brownie". I didn't care. I never cared what names people called me. They also called me "Hopalong Cassidy", at one time; because I walked with a "limp". The reason being was that my right leg was 1/8 inch shorter than my left leg. I used to practice walking so that people could not detect the leg length discrepancy. Most of the time, I covered the discrepancy very well–when tired–not so well. I would not let the "peer pressure" get to me. I liked me, and that was all that mattered. I wasn't necessarily a leader; however, you could never coerce me into being a follower of people that I considered to be trouble-makers. When we used to go to Bethany Center and two people got into a fight, the Center Director would put boxing gloves on the two opponents, and he let them do some "sparring" until they got tired. Then he took the boxing gloves off of them, and told them to go home and come back when both of them could behave themselves. This was a good way to get frustration out of their systems when the fellows would keep on complaining and fussing about each other.

I remember one day when my brother, Sage got home from school late from practicing sports. He made, what he thought was a "hamburger patty". My Mother noticed his supper was still in the refrigerator and she said, "Why didn't you eat your food that I left for you?" He said, "I did eat it." "I cooked that hamburger, put onions, mustard and catsup on it to "dress it up". My Mother looked in the "fridge" and discovered that Sage ate the dog food. My Mother said, "Oh my goodness, boy, you ate the wrong thing, and you're going to get sick!" We waited to see if he died. He did not die. We later teased him about it. We laughed at him until we cried. He then said, "Aaaah", I ate it, and it was good. All of us laughed about it for many, many years.

Who can forget our Assemblies held in the school auditorium. I can well remember Billy playing the accordion. O boy could he play that instrument! Remember "Bobby" with the strong voice singing, "The Lord's Prayer?" Everyone delighted in his singing. Then there was

Naomi, as usual dancing with those black-laced stockings with her straw hat on. Her dancing reminded you of the dancers back in the cowboy days. She dazzled the audience. Then there was Donna standing in the curve of the baby grand piano singing one of her favorite songs, I suppose. It was "O sirrah, sirrah, whatever "twill be, twill be" rendition. She looked and sang like a movie star. I wonder where she is today. How about our classmate, June who roller-skated on the stage. I was told that she won a lot of trophies. She was a beautiful skater. Then there were the girls with the batons doing their "twirling". They were throwing the batons up in the air and catching them while they were "twirling". That was great! We can't forget about Nancy and Dolores tap-dancing to the tune of the Dark Town Strutters Ball. Boy could they tap-dance–no doubt about it. We had people doing acrobats and girls dancing in a chorus line. We can't forget about Earl playing the tuba and bursting out all of our ear drums. No one could ever forget about Jesse playing the piano maestoso–one of those Bach or Chopin numbers. The songs she played should have been played with a symphony orchestra. She "brought the house down" when she played! She really did! Let's not forget about me. It was my turn to play my violin on the stage. I was accompanied by someone on the piano, I can't recall. The song that I played was called, "No Other Love". I can't believe that I can still remember that. What I can remember, too, is that a couple of my strings loosened, and I did the best I could and ended up playing with less than four (4) violin strings to finish my song. I believe the audience caught the drift of my plight, and when I finished playing, they gave me a standing ovation. What a day! That's all I can say.

Aside from the aforementioned entertainment, I have to clue you in on another project. The project was book report time. I always raised my hand to give my book report first. That could never happen, because the minute that I stood in front of the class they whistled, clapped, applauded and carried on just awful. Finally the teacher told them to "cut it out". She then took me aside, and asked me if I would do my book report after all of the others had finished theirs. After all the book reports were finished, and a few weeks had elapsed, finally I was able to give my book report. The fact that I was the Comedienne of my class, the "class clown", of course did not help–not at all. I produced good work; I was not disobedient or exhibited bad conduct. I enjoyed school, because although we had some difficult subjects, I made it fun.

Going to school for twelve years with the same people made it seem like a second family to me. When I finally graduated from school, that night, I felt like I was going to a funeral, because I knew we would be migrating from one another. This for me, was very hard. I always treated my classmates with humility and respect; and although, I kept only a few close friends, at a time, I never had any real problem getting along with any of them.

There comes a time when one person or another is exposed to "peer pressure". Today, it's an unhealthy situation. Due to the fact that I do not understand it, especially in this day and time, I try not to give my own personal opinion as to how I feel about it. My reason being that I do not want to be put into a class of people viewed as those who minimize the dangers of "peer pressure". It is very sad to me when we have to "stoop" so low as to degrade and make fun of people. We should not have to put up with those who malign individuals and call it fun. It is a despicable act and we should not tolerate those who engage in this type of conduct. A person's race, religion, or physical stature should not be attacked by others at anytime. Who cares whose "skinny", fat, short, having freckles, or who is bald. An individual may exhibit facial or body disfigurements or visual abnormalities from no fault of their own. If it were not for the "grace of God", that disability could be ours to wear. Once again we need to remember the good rule, "Do unto others as you would have them do unto you". If we would remember that the world could be so much better to live in. So what if you're so "darn" good looking. There's always going to come a time when you'll see someone much better looking than you. Sometimes the good looking people get ugly, and the ugly looking people get good looking. I've seen it happen many times, and so have you. You've seen heavy people get thinner and you've seen thin people get heavier. Regardless as to how you feel about the foregoing statements, allow me to share another story with you. When I was in the ninth grade, I was terribly "skinny". I really looked awful! I admit that. I was so thin that my Mother gave me spoonfuls of Scotts Emulsion and Cod Liver Oil and everything she could think of to help me gain more weight. She said that she wanted to put more meat on my bones. Children in the depression years had no weight problems–no way. Most of the children were thin–a few were fat. I assume that the reason for that was because there were no preservatives and/or additives put into our food to increase the life expectancy of the food.

However, one day when I came to school, the kids were teasing me about how thin I was, and the fact that I had a very small chest (if you know what I mean). I just brushed it off. I hardly cared about what they thought about the way I looked. I had more important things on my mind. I wanted that A or B in my classes. I wanted to further my education. A couple of days later, the girls gave me a gift all wrapped up in a beautiful package. I opened it up, and it was a beautiful red sweater and an artificial "prosthesis" (if you know what I mean) for me to wear under the sweater. Everyone "roared", and had a good laugh that day. The very next day, I wore the bright red sweater and the artificial prosthesis under the sweater to school and "strolled" into the classroom with it on. Everyone laughed and laughed. They didn't think I had the nerve to do it. They wanted to improve my looks, and at the same time "tease" me for my visual body defect, and I "went for it." That's the way I killed my "peer pressure". I think the kids appreciated me by accepting the joke that they played on me by just moving beyond it. I was voted the "Comedienne of the Class of 1953. "Sticks and stones can break your bones". Names do nothing!

TO THE READERS

I have succinctly given you, the readers, an adaptation of our lives as seen through a child's mind. This account was recalled to my memory decades later. However, all the information in the story was authenticated. Possibly this story may contain errors due to the fact that I have written this story by memory only. My account of this story, of course, is not infallible, by any means, but it will not take away the enjoyment of your reading this story. As an authoress, sharing this experience with you has given me a release of exhilaration and fulfillment and happiness and a sense of gratification in writing this book.

In conclusion I would like to share with you two prayers that we were taught to say each morning and evening.

Our morning prayer was:

> Father we thank you for the night and for the blessed
> morning light. For birds and food and loving care,
> And all that makes the world so fair.
>
> Help us to do the things we should, and be to others
> both kind and good, in all we do and in all we say,
> To be more loving every day.
>
> Amen

Our evening prayer was:

> Now I lay me down to sleep, I pray the Lord my soul to keep
>
> If I should die before I wake, I pray the Lord my soul to take
>
> Bless "Mommy", "Daddy", Aunt "Nanny" and Uncle "Fathead" all my brothers and sisters and all the people in the whole wide world.
>
> Amen

I need to state that I received fine educational training from Pottstown High School.

We had excellent teachers–teachers that made you want to learn. I feel that I grasped a wonderful command of the English language, because I had exceptional English teachers.

The knowledge that I gained through the Pottstown School District allowed me to secure excellent job opportunities, that enabled my husband and me to allow my children to attend college and other schools of higher learning.

With the proper educational training that I had in school, prepared me to manage my home after my husband passed away leaving me with three (3) children to finish raising. For this, I am forever grateful to the Pottstown School District.

I am eternally grateful to God, my redeemer–the preface of my being, still at my side, and still in my heart for his grace, mercy and loving kindness and blessings that he continues to bestow on me each and every day of my life. I also thank him for giving me loving parents that made sacrifices and provisions for me throughout my entire life. Hopefully, you the readers, have had an opportunity to peek into our lives, back in time; and I hope that the strange happenings brought some laughter to you as you read my story about our lives on "Chicken Hill," in Pottstown, Pa. "Adieu."

ABOUT THE AUTHOR

Arsonia M. (Glenn) Leisure was born in Pottstown, PA. She comes from a family of five brothers and four sisters. She is the third eldest child of the late Reverend and Mrs. Isaiah E. Glenn. She has a great love for writing, as well as a special love for playing her violin from time to time. This book entitled, "The Legend of Chicken Hill" is the second book that the author has written. Her first book, "London's Test of Love" was presented to the public in February, 1999. That book was a story about her son, London's battle with cancer and subsequent death. "The Legend of Chicken Hill" chronicles people living in a section of a town who had a struggle because of wartime. The story begins and deals with the aftermath of the 1929 Depression.

The author is a versatile person, and was able to gain entrance into many variables in her life. She loves people regardless of their ethnic backgrounds. Her first ambition was to become a Journalist. Due to the lack of financial aid, at the time of her graduation from high school, she made a second choice. That choice was to work in the business world, because she liked the "hustle and bustle" of that vocation. In the course of events, she chose office work. In addition to the business world, Arsonia chose to be a writer. She is multi-talented, and has multiple stories to share with her readers.

She feels that this book, could be listed "categorical" as a pragmatic phenomenon. It is definitely a motivational book describing the moves and actions of people in various life situations. The book is "light-hearted", religious, historical, and educational. It is also descriptive in the fields of psychology, youth, economics and science.

It covers nature, struggles, family values, memoirs and yet carries with it a "spin-off" of humor that was a part of our daily lives. The contents in the stories seem almost unbelievable. This, of course, makes the book quite enjoyable to read. She hopes that you will turn the pages of her book to read about things that happened in the days of "yore".

The Author is noted and appreciated for the following accomplishments:

- A 1954 Graduate of Pottstown High School,
  Pottstown, PA
- Awarded the Key to the City of West Chester, PA
  by the Mayor, 2001
- Pottstown High School Alumni Honoree, 2001
- Board Member - Alliance For a Clean Environment
- Joyce Reddick Black Heritage Award - 1999
- Environmental Advisory Board - Borough of Pottstown
- American Cancer Society Relay For Life Team Captain
- Mentor/Tutor - Pottstown School District
  (Golden Sage Program)
- Mentor (RSVP) Retired Senior Volunteer Program
- Board Member (PASC) Pottstown Area Seniors Center
- Night-Time Receptionist at a Nursing Home
- Member of the Writers Guild of America (East)
  New York City
- Member of (PARSE) PA Association of Retired
  State Employees

- Employment–Clerk/Typist and Clerk/Stenographer, II (Civil Service)
- Retired from the Pennsylvania Department of Health and Welfare with twenty-eight (28) years of dedicated and meritorious service to the people of Pennsylvania on August 2, 1996
- Author–"London's Test of Love" by Duncan & Duncan, Incorporated, February, 1999
- Poet: Is listed in the American Poetry Anthology, 1983 edition by John Frost, Santa Cruz, California
- She has appeared on her local (PCTV) television, as well as Channel 69, Channel 3 and 10 TV speaking against environmental pollution as an activist.
- Marital Status (W) Has three children, Lannette Suarez-Gnekre, Junius P. Leisure, II and London Kyle Leisure (now deceased)
- Eight grandchildren and four great-grandchildren
- Member Second Baptist Church

Made in the USA
Middletown, DE
04 December 2024

66099453R00040